Asperger Syndrome
– What Teachers
Need to Know

by the same author

Successful School Change and Transition for the Child with Asperger Syndrome
A Guide for Parents
Clare Lawrence
ISBN 978 1 84905 052 4

How to Make School Make Sense
A Parents' Guide to Helping the Child with Asperger Syndrome
Clare Lawrence
Foreword by Tony Attwood
ISBN 978 1 84310 664 7

of related interest

Working with Asperger Syndrome in the Classroom
An Insider's Guide
Gill D. Ansell
ISBN 978 1 84905 156 9

From Home to School with Autism
How to Make Inclusion a Success
K.I. Al-Ghani and Lynda Kenward
Illustrated by Haitham Al-Ghani
ISBN 978 1 84905 169 9

Asperger Syndrome in the Inclusive Classroom
Advice and Strategies for Teachers
Stacey W. Betts, Dion E. Betts and Lisa N. Gerber-Eckard
Foreword by Peter Riffle
ISBN 978 1 84310 840 5

Common SENse for the Inclusive Classroom
How Teachers Can Maximise Existing Skills to Support Special Educational Needs
Richard Hanks
ISBN 978 1 84905 057 9

Asperger Syndrome – What Teachers Need to Know

Second Edition

Matt Winter

with Clare Lawrence

Jessica Kingsley *Publishers*
London and Philadelphia

First edition published in 2003
This edition published in 2011
by Jessica Kingsley Publishers
116 Pentonville Road
London N1 9JB, UK
and
400 Market Street, Suite 400
Philadelphia, PA 19106, USA

www.jkp.com

Library of Congress Cataloging in Publication Data
Winter, Matt.
 Asperger syndrome : what teachers need to know / Matt Winter with Clare
Lawrence. -- 2nd ed.
   p. cm.
 Includes bibliographical references and index.
 ISBN 978-1-84905-203-0 (alk. paper)
 1. Asperger's syndrome in children. 2. Asperger's syndrome in children--
Patients--Education. I. Lawrence, Clare. II. Title.
 RJ506.A9W536 2011
 618.92'858832--dc22
                                             2010051329
British Library Cataloguing in Publication Data
A CIP catalogue record for this book is available from the British Library

ISBN 978 1 84905 203 0

Printed and bound in the United States of America

Contents

Introduction

As a teacher I understand how valuable a teacher's time is. When I needed to learn about Asperger Syndrome (AS), I discovered that I would have to wade through many substantial books written from a parental or psychological perspective, not from a teacher's point of view. After many hours of reading literature on AS, talking with parents of children with AS, discussions with professionals, experience as a classroom teacher and experience working with children with AS, I have been encouraged to write this condensed book to help save teachers' time.

The aim of the book is to provide you, the reader, with a summary of the information currently available on AS that is relevant to teachers, and to provide you with a better understanding of your AS students, quick tips and practical ideas that you can start using straight away in your class.

I hope that reading this gives you a good initial grounding and that you will be motivated to pursue further reading on the subject. At the end of the book there is a list of recommended reading and websites that highlight the sources I have found most useful. I hope you find this book valuable.

You will see that I have used gender pronouns interchangeably throughout the book. This is deliberate. Although AS is more prevalent in males than females, I have used both pronouns to show a balanced approach to those with AS.

Chapter 1

What is Asperger Syndrome?

Asperger Syndrome (AS) is a neuro-developmental difference that falls within the autistic spectrum. It is sometimes referred to as high functioning autism (particularly in the USA), and though it is often suggested that this is a different condition, from a teacher's point of view the two definitions are for practical teaching purposes interchangeable. AS is characterized by difficulty with four main areas:

1. Social interaction.

2. Communication.

3. Imagination (e.g. imagining what others are thinking).

4. Sensory sensitivity (e.g. to bright light, noise, textures, tastes, touch, smells).

Lorna Wing (Burgoine and Wing 1983) described the main clinical features of AS as:

- lack of empathy
- naïve, inappropriate, one-sided interaction
- little ability to form or maintain peer friendships
- pedantic, repetitive speech
- poor non-verbal communication
- intense absorption in certain subjects
- clumsy and ill-coordinated movements and odd postures.

Personally, I believe this puts a very negative spin on the syndrome and I prefer to think of it differently, in a more positive light. Some of the positive traits commonly associated with AS are:

- honesty
- reliability
- original thinking
- dedication
- determination.

It is fairly common for children with AS to also be diagnosed with other syndromes or conditions. Over 70 per cent of young people with a diagnosis of Autism Spectrum Disorder have an additional mental health problem (National Autistic Society 'You Need to Know' campaign 2010).

Some common ones are:

- *Attention Deficit Hyperactivity Disorder (ADHD/ ADD)* – an inability to maintain concentration, even when trying her hardest.

- *Depression* – probably the most common mental health problem. Clinical depression is a persistent depressive state beyond normal daily emotions.

- *Dysgraphia* – difficulty putting thoughts into writing, particularly while trying to read the board or listen to someone talk at the same time.

- *Dyslexia* – difficulty with decoding single words, making reading, writing and spelling difficult.

- *Dyspraxia* – a neurologically based impairment or immaturity of the organization of movement. This can affect a person's coordination, making him appear clumsy or unable to write neatly. It may also impact on a person's language development, his perception and his ability to organize his thoughts.

- *Echolalia* – a tendency to mimic other people's speech.

- *Obsessive Compulsive Disorder (OCD)* – a disorder where people develop obsessions and/or compulsions (senseless repetitive actions) that they perform in an effort to reduce discomfort and anxiety. These obsessions and compulsions become all-encompassing and intrude on the person's life.

Tony Attwood has described AS as a different way of approaching life, one that is dominated by the pursuit of knowledge and truth. The way AS may present itself in your classroom is explored in the next chapter.

Chapter 2

What Signs Might a Child Display?

One of the aspects of AS that makes it difficult to get to grips with is that it presents itself in many different ways. No two children with AS will have exactly the same set of symptoms. Below is a list of the possible signs a child with AS might display and the ways in which she might behave. Keep in mind that each child displays each sign to a different extent, in a different way, and may well not display some at all. The signs may also come in waves – a certain sign might not be prominent for a while but can return later on. Many are more likely to become apparent if the child is stressed, anxious or tired.

General
Honest

- Will not understand why people lie.
- Will say exactly what she thinks.

- Will stick loyally by people.

- Learns to lie later than her peers, and when she does will often be an unconvincing liar, often without awareness of the transparency of the lie.

Creative

- Often approaches a problem from a completely different angle from the rest of the class.

- Prefers to use methods that he devises himself to solve problems, rather than conventional methods.

- Can genuinely find it hard to distinguish fiction from reality.

- May have unexpected talents, for example may be musical, artistic or good at drama.

Special interests

- May develop a topic or couple of topics of intense special interest.

- May add new special interests from time to time.

- Wants to find out all she can on the current topic.

- May be extremely knowledgeable about topics of special interest and can often communicate about them in an adult way.

- The special interest(s) often can be a 'safe zone' as she feels more secure when immersed in her interest.

Enjoys routines

- Responds well to set routines – likes to know what to expect during the school day.

- Dislikes deviation from routines and may become upset by unexpected changes of lesson or teacher.

- Can create many routines of his own to put some order back into his life.

- If there is an order to a routine, he does not like the order to be changed.

Social interaction
Difficulty reading social cues and body language

- May interrupt conversations at inappropriate times.

- Does not pick up on verbal or non-verbal signals that a person has had enough of the conversation.

- Will often act the same in different social situations (e.g. always very formal) and in the same way to different people (e.g. peers and school principal or head teacher).

- Can appear rude through using wrong means of address (e.g. says 'Excuse me' but sounds sarcastic).

- Can misinterpret polite conversation or greetings as signs of real interest or friendships.

- Is eager to make friends but appears 'socially clumsy'.

- Misses the meaning of sarcasm when used by others.

- Often misinterprets facial expressions.

- Finds the concept of taking turns difficult to put into practice.

Difficulty expressing/modulating her emotions

- May get more emotional than situation seems to warrant.

- May not be able to recognize when stress levels are rising (no 'early warning system') so can suddenly find herself in a particularly stressed or anxious state.

- May appear unmoved when in fact is profoundly upset or disturbed.

- Can appear to have a quick temper or be unpredictable because something slight may be the 'last straw'.

- Finds it hard to restrain impulsive thoughts or actions.

- May laugh inappropriately when she doesn't understand the situation.

- May express inappropriate emotions (e.g. may laugh in a sad situation, or cry in a happy one).

- May experience intense fear because she cannot predict a likely safe outcome.

- May find it difficult to distinguish emotions (e.g. sad from angry).

Difficulty reading other people's emotions

- Will listen to what is said but fails to interpret correctly the facial expression of the person, and misses the tone it was said in, so only partially understands message.

- May believe that others share same emotion. For example, may not understand that own happiness does not mean everyone else is feeling happy too.

- May understand that someone else is happy or sad but may not know how to respond appropriately.

Strong moral code and sense of justice

- Has a need for things to be fair.

- Once a value is adopted, can get very upset when other people disregard it.

- Gets upset when other people ignore rules and may become a rule enforcer.

- Easily 'wound up' by others due to this inflexible view of right and wrong.

Theory of mind[1] difficulties

- Has trouble working out what another person might be thinking.

- Has difficulty working out a person's motivation.

---

1   Theory of mind refers to the notion that many individuals with Autistic Spectrum Disorders do not understand that other people have thoughts, ideas and ways of thinking that are different from theirs. They therefore also have difficulty understanding the attitudes, actions and emotions of others (Edelson 1995).

- Can at times assume, and work on the basis, that everyone thinks and feels the same as he does about things.

- May assume that other people know everything he knows so fails to supply information.

- Can do things and not realize he is hurting the feelings of someone else.

- May have difficulty with literacy tasks involving passages about people's motivation and inferred emotions.

- Will often completely believe that he is 100 per cent right.

Controlled play

- Needs to be in control of games.

- Has a tendency to play games that mimic reality, a film or a computer game.

- Has little interest in (or understanding of) games that he does not control.

- Tends to be happier with non-competitive games.

- May have an intense imagination for the world of his own games to the point where they 'blot out' reality.

- Play can remain imaginative and 'childish' into adolescence, making young person target for ridicule.

Physical/senses
Motor clumsiness

- May have odd gait when walking.

- May display complicated and repetitive hand or arm movements or have specific routines he likes to repeat.

- Often has difficulty with tasks that require fine motor skills (e.g. tying shoe laces).

- Often finds handwriting difficult and will therefore have messy writing or be unable to handwrite at all.

- May find ball sports and balancing activities difficult.

- May become more obviously affected by motor clumsiness in adolescence.

- Tends to dislike and find difficult competitive team sports.

Rhythm

- May have a fantastic ear for rhythm when playing by herself.

- May find it very difficult to keep a rhythm with others.

- Could find rhythm both comforting and/or highly frustrating.

Sensory sensitivity

- May be far more sensitive to sensory input than other children.

- May find certain smells, sounds, lights or tastes unpleasant to the point of being a torture

- May be physically ill when she smells a certain smell or really physically hurt if she is touched.

- May be also be *insensitive* to some sensory stimuli so, for example, may appear deaf or may not notice minor injuries.

VISUAL

- Bright light can be unbearable.

- Flickering light (even if very minor and not noticed by others) can be incredibly distracting and irritating.

- May be fascinated by certain lights.

- May find it physically unpleasant to read certain text.

- May dislike being looked at – it has been said 'I feel as if the person will see inside me'.

AUDITORY

- High-pitched, sudden or loud noises can be unbearable or highly distracting.

- Fear of sudden loud noises may be an intense distraction in itself. Knowing an alarm *may* go off can mean little else is taken in.

- May hear things before other people.
- May hear things others don't hear at all or don't notice (e.g. the sound of an electric light).

TACTILE

- May intensely dislike the feel of some fabrics, especially in clothing.
- May find the feel of labels in clothing very unpleasant.
- May find it painful or unpleasant to be touched, especially on certain areas of the body.
- May be very sensitive to the discomfort caused by restrictive clothing (e.g. may feel 'strangled').
- May be intensely drawn to some tactile sensations, especially when seeking to relax. May seek weight or deep pressure, so burrows under mats or clothing. May seek to hide in small, enclosed spaces.
- May be impervious to certain sensations, including heat, cold and minor injuries.

OLFACTORY

- Strong odours, particularly perfumes, can overwhelm.
- May often be the first to smell something.
- May intensely dislike particular smells.

- May be reassured or comforted by certain smells and may hold objects or clothing with these smells up to her face.

Poor sense of direction

- Needs lots of visual landmarks included in directions.
- May struggle to remember left and right.
- May be confused by apparently minor changes (e.g. a table being repositioned or a wall display being altered).
- Some children with AS can develop an excellent long-term memory of a place once these landmarks are established. May only need one familiarization visit and will instantly be able to find way around next time.
- Confusion may be caused by misunderstanding of the directions used rather than poor directional sense. For example, a child told to go to 'Mr Smith's Room' may understand this as being the room where the pupil first encountered Mr Roberts rather than the room he normally teaches in. Time should be spent to 'unpick' confusions.

Bilateral co-ordination difficulties

- Finds it hard to move both sides of the body in harmony.
- May, as a result, find writing and ball skills difficult.

Visual perception difficulties

- Can find it hard to distinguish an object from the background.

- Has difficulty working out proximity of an object or the speed it is travelling, which can cause poor road safety awareness.

- May have difficulty recognizing differences in faces, so may find it hard to identify different individuals.

- Has difficulty identifying distinct differences in similar objects.

- Can find it extremely difficult to look at someone when talking as there is so much visual and aural information to process at the same time.

- May have difficulty using stairs or steps because of visual disorientation.

- May find it difficult to negotiate a crowded environment, especially one where people are changing direction frequently and rapidly (e.g. crowded yard or hallways).

Aural perception problems

- May find it difficult to distinguish one sound (e.g. a teacher speaking) from background noise.

- May find it difficult to 'filter out' a background noise. The whirr of a projector or the buzzing of the air conditioning unit may be overwhelming.

- May find it difficult to interpret words as meaningful language.

- May find it difficult to understand what is being said if there are competing sensory stimuli (e.g. a background colour or a strong smell can 'blot out' words).

- May appear 'deaf' to sounds if absorbed in an activity.

High pain threshold

- May not appear to feel low levels of pain.

- Can be over- and under-sensitive to temperature.

- May express the feeling of pain through behaviour. For example, if a child has an injury or illness she may become irritable and uncooperative when you interact with her instead of complaining about it as other children would. She may be unaware of the cause of her behaviour.

High stress levels

- Social, communication and sensory difficulties place large demands on the child and he often has high stress levels as a result.

- Particularly when most stressed, may be prone to repeating things over and over.

- If aware he has made a public error, he may get upset by this but be unaware of how to fix it.

- Can quickly become physically and mentally tired as a result of high stress levels.

- May retreat into 'inner world' and miss much of what is going on around him.

Chapter 3

What are some General Strategies for the Classroom?

The list of symptoms in the previous chapter may seem overwhelming. Remember that each child will only have a subset of these. The good news is that there are some strategies you can employ with the whole class that could help most of your students.

You may well have implemented many of these strategies in your classroom already. Remind yourself of their particular importance for children with AS. See if you can generalize new strategies for the whole class. Be inventive and keep on trying.

Above all else, maintain consistency in the classroom. These children need plenty of structure and will react negatively to changes. Keep your sense of humour and remember it is OK to have a laugh!

Make everything visual

Remember that many of these children are visual learners. Any visual link you can make will help the child with AS, and visual cues and plans can be very useful. These can be sophisticated, like a visual organizer (see Chapter 8), or very simple. A sketched 'countdown chart' that you gradually rub out to the end of an activity ('That's half your time gone!') can be a tremendous help to the child with AS in understanding how long is left on an activity. Boxes on worksheets can indicate both where to write and roughly how long an answer is expected to be. A written summary of the lesson content and structure that can be pre-viewed by the older student can vastly increase understanding. The flip-side of this is the need to avoid visual distractors. Some children with AS cannot help reading and re-reading posters and wall displays, and even information such as safety notices (which are to all intents and purposes invisible to most students) can be something a pupil with AS cannot help but take in.

Warn about changes

Give the child as much advance warning about changes to the scheduled day as possible. Give him a reason for the change and where possible give a visual indication (a timetable change or an alteration to the visual schedule). Talk him through the situation and tell him exactly what will be required. Rehearse any new activity with him if you can, and allow an 'out' if the situation cannot be adequately prepared (see safe area p.43). For older students you may be able to use email or a page on your school website to warn about significant changes as early as possible.

Make sure that you emphasise what is not changing as well. For example, make sure it is clear that, although a different teacher is expected, the lesson will still be in the same classroom, the seating will remain the same and the same homework schedule will be followed.

Make lists and schedules

Create lists of tasks to be done. Assign times by which each will be carried out, so that progress can be monitored. As with change (above), use technology to support the child with AS. Email assignments home, allow use of a palm top or similar to record information and check that longer work is progressing to prevent build-up of anxiety. For the younger child, break a task down into simple steps and make it clear when each has been completed successfully. Lists, for example, of equipment to be packed in the school bag, can make a tremendous difference. These may be picture-matches for the youngest child, or a check-list for the older. Each is both making the pupil more efficient and providing him with strategies that work into later life.

Colour code

Use colours, and possibly strong visual symbols, to indicate different areas of the classroom, and different activities. The blue shelf may be where maths equipment is kept. The red shelf is where language materials are, etc. Make sure the labelling is clear. If possible, extend this throughout the school, so that different areas of the school have different colours or visual codes that are easy to recognize. For the older child, colour-coded subject folders can help with organization, as can colour-coding on both timetables and plans of schools. However, as with so many things, be aware of the inherent dangers in this system. How will the child feel if he is expected to sit at the 'red' science table to do his spelling test, or if his French class is relocated to Room 6, shaded blue for History on his plan?

Do things as you talk

The child with AS will often appear to be very inattentive when people are talking. She does not gain much from body language and does not naturally look at people when they are talking. In this case it can actually help her *not* to look at you.

The opposite can also be true. A child with AS might not take in anything you say even if she appears to be looking at you and listening, or she may only pick out certain words or phrases from a conversation. She may become 'blocked' by one thing you say, or misunderstand or misinterpret. Always check understanding and try never to take anything for granted. For example, she may have encyclopaedic knowledge of the planets of the solar system, but be unable to answer the simplest question if you refer to a meteor rather than a meteorite.

If you can, do something that is visually interesting while relating to what you are talking about. For example, use a model or create a diagram. This will encourage the child to look at you and begin to pick up on body language. It will also help her remember what you are talking about by tying the concept to something visual, which is more easily recalled.

Use timers

Often a child with AS will have a poor sense of time. Use an egg timer or a similar, easy-to-follow device to set the amount of time for a task. Point out what he needs to have finished by specific times. If you use this strategy, stick to it. Do not expect him to work past the timer. Praise him when he completes the required work. Encourage him to beat his output from last time. In this way he is working in competition with himself, not with the other children in the class. Similarly, a 'five minute warning' to a change of activity can be great at helping a child with AS accepting that he is going to have to stop what he is doing.

Create formal rules

Many pupils with AS find it very difficult to make sense of social learning activities. Having clear and consistent rules for the class can help considerably, especially if they are written down and displayed. These may be 'rules' such as putting a hand up rather than shouting out, or only speaking through the Chair (now there's a confusing term for the person with AS!) during class discussions. Other tactics include using a speaking ball or other object that gets passed around to the person who is allowed to speak. Explicit techniques such as these help the child with AS to learn to take turns and not interrupt, and also make it clearer who she should be attending to.

Use teacher selected groups

Always use teacher selected groups for activities – this ensures that the child will not be left out. Because of their difficulties with social interaction, and particularly with competitive team sport, children with AS may not be 'picked' by their classmates to join teams or groups. Teacher selected groups allow for you to separate the child with AS from 'trouble spots' and to ensure he is working with pupils who are likely to be more tolerant and accepting of his differences.

Use teacher selected seating

In a similar way, it can help the pupil with AS if you provide a seating plan for your class. Deciding where to sit can cause considerable anxiety for the child with AS, and places that are 'taken' or 'saved' can lead to feelings of social rejection.

One of the most important considerations when choosing where to seat a child with AS is her sensory sensitivities. In addition you need to take into account the distractions in different areas of the room. Some children might actually prefer to face a wall or a window (so long as the scene outside is not interesting) so they do not notice the other children as much. The pupil should be somewhere that gives her sufficient space, that is easy to access in order to give help and that has an easy path through to the 'safe area' (see p.43) should she need to use it.

Encourage controlled interaction

You probably use lots of cooperative learning strategies in your class already. They are a good way to encourage all children to interact, and can be of huge benefit to the child with AS. The 'think, pair, share' model is particularly good, involving giving students time to think about a problem, then explaining their thoughts to a partner before feeding back to the class. This model allows for more thinking time and greater participation, and answering the question with their partners often gives children more courage to speak out to the whole class. Most of all, the predictable structure is likely to be appealing to the pupil with AS.

When you first introduce these strategies remember that, even though they are structured, they can still be challenging to someone with AS. The large amount of one-on-one social interaction might be quite threatening. Introduce this social learning slowly, and give the pupil with AS plenty of chances to get used to it. You could perhaps use a topic that you know the child with AS will find easy to talk about and use it to practise the strategy before it is used during a lesson. You may also want to teach the strategy to the child before teaching it to the class so that he is more familiar with it.

Monitor your speech

Check that when giving instructions:

- your voice is the primary sound and is not competing against background noise
- you pause between sentences to allow processing time
- not too much information is given out in one go – only one instruction at a time
- you avoid metaphorical questions which can distract as the answer is sought
- you avoid sarcasm or hints at meaning
- you explain metaphors and other figures of speech
- your instruction is unambiguous
- you only say, 'Will you?' and 'Can you?' if there actually is a choice.

Sometimes you will have verbal habits you don't even realize. It can be really useful to have a peer observe a lesson and take notes on your verbal instructions and explanations.

Repeat instructions

It is always important to check that the pupil with AS really has understood instructions. You could get various children in the class to repeat back the instructions given to increase repetition, but be aware that rephrased instructions may seem like new instructions to the child with AS. It may be more useful to get the child with AS to come to you before going to his desk to repeat back what he is going to do. Make sure that he knows not just what to do and how to do it, but also where, when and how much is required. An open-ended instruction such as 'Write down what you did in the holidays' can really throw a child with AS, who doesn't know what to include and what to leave out.

Be prescriptive

Very often a pupil with AS will struggle to 'know what to do' in school. Other pupils seem to know through instinct that several pupils gathered outside a classroom means line up before you enter. They know when a teacher has finished his preamble and they are expected to get on with the task. They know that the sound of a bell means come in from break or that a whistle means stand still. Very few of the expectations of school culture are ever made clear, but for the pupil with AS this can mean a thousand confusions every day. If your pupil looks lost, give a direct instruction that leaves no doubt. It may feel rather old-fashioned to instruct a student to 'Wait there until you are told to come in' or 'Look to the front of the classroom', but this may be precisely the level of clarity that the student needs. Above all, never assume that behaviour is defiant until you are absolutely sure that the student knows what to do to behave correctly. If the child with AS is still wandering around the room when everyone else is sitting down working, it may be that he is not being difficult nor even indicating stress. It may just be that no-one has told him to sit down!

Chapter 4

What are some Individual Strategies for the Pupil?

Because every child with AS is unique, there is no foolproof list of strategies that will work for everyone. Below are some ideas that have been tried and found to be successful with certain children with AS. Choose ones that you think might benefit the child you are working with and give them a try.

Create a school map

If the child is having trouble navigating the school or working out where he is allowed to go, create a colour-coded map (see Colour code p.29). Have a certain colour for areas where the child may only go with a teacher's permission or in an emergency. Do not say to him there are areas he 'cannot go to', as he might take this literally even in extreme situations.

Arrange for an early arrival

If the child is having trouble organizing herself at the start of the day or settling down, arrange for her to arrive at school early. Have a place where she can go (e.g. library) where she can relax and adjust to being at school before heading to class. Similarly, if an older child finds the crush and bustle of managing the time between lessons distressing, allow her to leave each lesson a little early so that she can make her way to her next class while the corridors are still empty.

Use her special interests

The child's special interests are a huge source of motivation for a child with AS. There are many ways that you can use this to your advantage:

- Relate the work you are doing to the special interest in some way. For example, if the special interest is aeroplanes and you are studying time in maths, you could base her work around airline timetables.

- Show her that what she is learning will help her when she wants to find out more information about her special interest.

- Use extra time investigating her special interest as a reward (e.g. when she completes certain activities, she can have ten minutes in the library).

- Make use of her special skills to give her status in the class (e.g. if she is big on computers, let her be a computer monitor who helps the other children with computers).

• Use the special interest as the subject if you are concentrating more on the 'how' than the 'what'. If the learning outcome is to make a presentation, write a newspaper report or compose a song, why not allow the special interest as the subject? You are likely to get a much better result, and the task is likely to be enjoyed by all parties.

Allow alternative note-taking methods

If the child has difficulty with handwriting, use a variety of methods of note taking. Material might be provided for the student in pre-viewed written form. The teacher aide and the student might share the writing (a dialogue, using question and answer can elicit very good results) or the aide might scribe for the pupil. You could provide a worksheet where keywords need to be written to fill in the gaps (i.e. cloze work). Above all, encourage use of word processing or computers. Few adults use handwriting except for their own note taking, and emphasis on developing neat handwriting skills is fast becoming outmoded. The emphasis must be on communicating and on the student being given every opportunity to show what he knows, rather than stumbling because of the lack of a particular (and increasingly unnecessary) skill.

Create a code for help

As many children with AS are very insecure about appearing stupid, invent a code that the child can use to ask for help without the other children realizing. He may place his pencil case a certain way on his desk or stretch in a particular way to indicate that he needs help. You can then approach him as if you are looking at his work and give him ideas or the support he is looking for.

Be patient when asking questions

When you ask a question, the child has to stop thinking her current thoughts, lock those away for later, decipher the question, formulate an answer and then respond. This may take a while. If you interrupt or try to finish sentences for her, she may have to start her thought processes over again. Don't expect her to look at you, as this may actually break her concentration.

Be directive

Remember that giving a child with AS a choice can be stressful. He can struggle for ages over which is the best choice and a decision means he has to risk getting it wrong. It may seem like a straightforward choice to you but it could feel like the biggest decision in the world for the child. While it is useful for the child to learn about choices, keep them easy and help him through them.

Respect 'time out'

Sometimes the child with AS may seem to withdraw and go into himself for a while. It is important to be aware that this is perfectly natural for him, and is probably doing him a world of good! This 'time out' may well actually help the child to cope with the stresses of the world around him, and as such you would do well to respect it to a certain extent. Try to balance your need for the child to be paying attention with his need to withdraw, and try to work with him on a balance that works for you both.

Agree an independent 'fall-back' activity

Your pupil will often need individual help to get started with a task, or to overcome problems as the task goes on. You and/or your teaching aide will no doubt work hard to support her, but the practical truth of the real world of the classroom is that you may not be free to give this help straight away. This may mean that she sits there not doing anything for periods of time.

Agree with your pupil on a 'fall-back' activity that she will return to if she is stuck. This could perhaps be reading a favourite book on the subject or completing a familiar-format workbook. This activity gives her something to do until you are able to provide the one-to-one input she requires. It prevents her from being disruptive or appearing idle and means that her time in class is always spent usefully. It also gives her something that is reassuring, familiar and successful to prevent the feeling that she is not coping.

Work on home/school links

Good communication between school and home is vital if the pupil with AS is going to thrive. For one thing, it is going to help him enormously if there can be consistency across the two environments (and bear in mind that AS exists across all social, ethnic and religious boundaries). If the accepted rule at home is to remove your shoes at the door, it is going to be difficult for the child with AS to feel comfortable wearing shoes in class. On a more day-to-day level, home must be able to communicate that the pupil has had a bad night, that he is distressed or anxious, or if any problems are developing. The school needs to be able to request support (e.g. to pack the school bag with the correct equipment), to flag up that changes are approaching or, in fact, just to make clear when things are going well. Fortunately we live in an age of communication. Emails, texts and phone calls can all be used as well as the more traditional home/school diary. It is important to bear in mind that the pupil with AS will almost certainly do better in his school life if you work with (and support) his parents.

Introduce an Exit Card

Introduce a card that can be presented to allow the pupil to move away from a stressful situation. The first skill that may be lost when a pupil with AS becomes overwhelmed is the ability to communicate. He may be unable to articulate that he is becoming distressed, and may instead resort to the simplest strategy to get away – a push or a punch. An Exit Card can be wonderful for preventing flare-ups.

Use a safe area

A safe area (often also called a haven or Quiet Room) is somewhere a pupil can move to in order to calm down and regain control. For the younger child this may be an area of the classroom such as the quiet corner or reading zone, or, for the older, it may be another room such as Learning Support or the library. It is important to bear in mind that if it is away from your room you will need to make sure that it is supervised and that there is a system in place to make sure that he has arrived there safely.

It can be helpful for the child if he can keep some of his own possessions in the safe area, particularly those to do with a current special interest. It is quite likely that time spent here, engaged in this activity, will be enough to allow the child to 'regroup' and either rejoin the previous activity or at least be able to articulate the problem (see Chapter 7, How Do I Help with the Child's Stress?).

Chapter 5

How Can I Help the Pupil with AS to Learn?

Often a pupil with AS may be using almost all his energy just to get through the day. He is dealing with sensory over-stimulation, social demands, changes of pace and subject, and a hundred misunderstandings and confusions. Given these, it is hardly surprising that academic under-achievement becomes a serious issue for some children with AS.

The other danger can come from the child being identified as having 'Special Needs'. Unfortunately this can sometimes cause people to inadvertently lower academic expectation even though a child with AS may in fact be exceptionally bright. Just like with all your students, it is important to try to find ways to challenge the pupil with AS while being mindful of increasing his stress.

That may, of course, seem easier said than done! How can the pupil be encouraged to do better without her self-esteem being damaged by feeling a 'failure'? How can her extra needs be accommodated while continuing to challenge her overall intelligence? How can her specific differences and strengths associated with her AS be used and brought into play?

The following are all aspects of AS that impact specifically on learning. They are questions to ask yourself, especially when you hit problems with enabling your pupil with AS to do as well as you feel she can. Awareness of these issues of AS can go a great way in compensating for them, and indeed your awareness of the strengths of the pupil's condition can help to allow the child to use them to her best advantage.

- *Are you sure he knows how to do the task?* A pupil with AS may not realize that he knows something if he has not been taught it in this particular subject or area. He will not instinctively be able to apply a skill learned in a different situation.

- *Are your instructions sufficiently clear?* A pupil with AS may fail to complete a task if instructions are not full and accurate (e.g. if 'turn over' is not written at bottom of page) or may complete a task too briefly if the detail required is not made clear (e.g. may answer 'Why do you think Hitler invaded Poland?' with 'Because it said so in my book').

- *Is he struggling with the concept of 'best alternative'?* He may find multi-choice questions difficult if he doesn't agree that any of the options is completely 'right'.

- *Is there a problem with thinking ahead?* He may find it hard to think through to the end of a task or to predict a safe outcome if a science experiment, for example, appears to be dangerous.

- *Is she struggling with choice?* If you find that your pupil seems to be rushing at her work without due consideration, it could be that she is panicking because of the choices. She may find it hard to choose between options so tends to make a rash choice or none at all. She may start with the first question on the list and not understand that there are alternatives.

- *Is he paralysed by the fear of failure?* Many pupils with AS have a disproportionate fear of criticism and of appearing stupid to others. Their self-image may be very much tied in to being 'clever', which makes them extremely sensitive to any criticism and may mean that they find failure absolutely crushing. You may need to work to positively encourage mistakes. Often children with AS need to learn that it is OK to make mistakes so long as they learn from them. Try to move the blame away from the pupil by saying that the task is really hard and you are pleased he is trying it. Say things like, 'I am glad you made that mistake because now I know that I need to teach you about it.'

- *Is he struggling with getting the words from his head down on paper?* Try different techniques to allow the pupil to show what he knows. Use a scribe to write for him and a laptop to help with the writing. Encourage techniques such as mind-mapping and presenting ideas visually. It may help if he speaks his thoughts aloud as he works. If so, don't stop him but encourage him to whisper. He may need to take examinations in a separate room away from distractions and where his whispering will not distract others.

- *Is she resisting the activity as 'pointless'?* A pupil with AS may not be able to infer 'the point' of a learning activity unless this is made very clear. Try giving her a brief plan at the start of the lesson so that she knows what to expect and also what the learning point is. Knowing what is going to happen can be deeply reassuring for the child with AS.

- *Is your teaching style not the best way for her to learn?* It can be hard for you as a teacher to really see things from the pupil with AS's point of view. Try experimenting with alternative learning and study methods. She may learn best through accessing a CD-Rom or the internet or through independent study (e.g. going to the library to gather information). She may learn through reading rather than through listening, or through doing rather than through listening. Keep searching together to find what works best for her.

Subject-specifics issues

Some aspects of AS will bring particular challenges and issues in particular subject areas. As the pupil grows up and moves to a school where teachers become more subject-specialized, an awareness of how AS affects individual subjects can be particularly useful.

For example, the pupil with AS:

- may not understand irony in literature
- may find learning and accessing words in a new language very difficult, especially if struggling with aspects of her own language
- may struggle with different viewpoints in history
- may literally 'see things differently', resulting in surprising or highly individual approaches to art
- may enjoy the 'absolutes' of science and maths and dislike the ambiguity of humanities subjects
- may have very definite beliefs and find study of other cultures and religions challenging
- may find music lessons actually painful due to auditory processing differences
- may be overwhelmed by the smells of cookery or chemistry
- may find the competitive element of physical education particularly distressing, or find the physical element impossible to manage.

Additionally, in any subject the pupil may dislike revising anything learned once and see it as a waste of time. He may also struggle when higher-level education contradicts lower. For example, learnt 'facts' such as 'It is impossible to take three away from two' may mean distress when negative numbers are taught.

Don't forget the strengths of AS!

There are, of course, many 'pluses' as well as 'minuses' to AS, and it is essential that you as a teacher keep these always in mind and do your best to help your pupils with AS to use them where they can.

Remember that the pupil with AS may:

- be able to recall large amounts of factual information

- have a very strong visual memory, tending to remember in pictures and scenes, even when language is her best skill

- recall things seen more easily than those heard. Her memory may be quite remarkably detailed and this can be a real asset if she is helped to use visual prompts, such as photographs from the school trip, to access it

- have original ways of approaching a problem. Don't assume that the way she is working is 'wrong'. When she has worked through the problem, get her to explain her method to you. Be prepared to let her use unconventional techniques and processes, as long as they work

- have a wide and unusual vocabulary and have an excellent knowledge of the exact meaning of words

- be a high achiever in topics that have a rigid structure to them

- be tremendously tenacious and pursue a problem's solution long after a neuro-typical child would give up

- have a strong moral code which means that teaching politics or ethics can be reinvigorated as a subject with real passion

- have a genuine and enthusiastic interest in the topic, should you happen to be studying something that is of particular interest to her. If you are, she may well know many things that you don't know and you may be able to use her knowledge as a new resource

- be able to recall things (particularly images) from her very early years or over a long time span. She may be the best person to ask if you are not sure exactly what happened in the previous lesson, or what you said about a topic last year or even several years ago

- have a completely new 'take' on a subject. All teachers can become jaded, especially if we teach the same topics and subject year after year. Having a pupil with AS in your class can be a tremendous help to you, on a personal level. You may find your ideas and expectations challenged and your way at looking at the subject completely turned around!

Chapter 6

What About Homework?

You may find that this issue causes the child (and you!) a disproportionate amount of stress. Children with AS tend to view school as the place to work, and home as the place to relax. Any suggestion to do work at home can cause great anxiety. Why should he be working at his place of rest? In addition, the strategies and interventions used at school to aid the child in his work may not be available at home. It is therefore really important that you discuss this topic with the child's parents at the earliest opportunity.

The issue of homework is further compounded by the fact that most children with AS require more 'down time' than their peers to recover from the day at school. They have been working twice as hard as the other students. Not only have they been doing all the school work, they have also been trying hard to decipher social situations, confusing statements, body language and facial expressions. They have also been coping with huge amounts of sensory stimulation and have been trying to adjust to unexpected changes in their routines. By the time school ends they are often physically and mentally exhausted. On top of all this, the child will often still be processing events from the day and will need time for his mind to 'wind down' so he can concentrate on something new.

With all these factors in mind, the question needs to be asked, 'Is the gain made from doing homework worth the amount of stress that is caused?' In many cases the ongoing battle may not be worth it for anyone.

Modify homework

If homework really is unavoidable, it needs to be modified to make the work as easy as possible – and as useful as possible – for the child. Often for the pupil with AS creative solutions need to be found.

- Make sure all homework instructions are written down. If you just give them verbally or add key information verbally to written instructions, the child is likely to be confused or not be able to remember it all. Ideally you will be able to email work to the child, ensuring it is useful to him and making sure that all details are clear.

- You, as the teacher, need to look through the homework that you set and decide what is really going to be of benefit to this child. Prioritize tasks and remove ones that are not going to be of much benefit. If you can, alter the main tasks so that they are more appealing to, and useful for, this particular child. For example, consider the case where a teacher is setting a research assignment on sea life. If the primary objective is for the child to practise researching then why can't he do research on one of his special interests instead? Conversely, if the primary objective is learning about sea life, can he read some books on the subject or watch a film about it (two easier tasks) instead?

- Tasks that are going to take more than one night to complete will most likely need monitoring. She could easily become confused at the beginning of the process and go off on a different tangent. She could bring her work to you after completing her initial plan and at each key stage for checking. At this point you should go over the expectations for the next stage again. This managing of longer tasks is a useful skill to develop.

Overall, though, it is important to remember that he may just be too exhausted to work after school. He may actively need to spend time in his 'own world'. That is learning too, and it is important that people respect that. Given all of these factors, is he actually going to benefit from doing homework at all?

Establish a homework environment

It may help the child who has to do homework to agree with his parents a dedicated homework location. He should not be required to do 'homework' outside of this place. It should be free from any distraction. Take time to think about sensory issues. For example, are there noises that will upset him?

Ask the parents to set definite start and end times to homework with scheduled break time in between. Work with them to create a reward system that is linked to the amount of work done in this time, not to how quickly he does a certain piece of work. This stops homework becoming never ending for both the child and the parents. Help him by prioritizing the work so that the most important tasks will be done first. This reward system may well be linked with doing some independent study on his real interests, even if that is only accessing computer game posting boards or looking for game cheats, finding out about solar flares or retrieving yet more statistics on traffic lights!

It is likely to be essential to have a computer available in the study place. As much homework as possible should be completed on this as the need to handwrite work can add extra pressure. It often takes a large amount of concentration to write legibly and therefore the child's focus is moved from their work to their writing.

If the child with AS is having real difficulty with the concept of doing schoolwork at home, you could investigate other places she could go to do it. Perhaps she could have a small break then work in the library after school. Perhaps she could join a homework club at lunchtimes? Perhaps there will be breaks in her timetable when you and the school together have looked at whether she needs to study the full range of subjects (see Chapter 11, section on Subject choices).

Support independent study

Although homework can be a pointless source of stress, older children do need to learn independent study habits. These can be encouraged and developed in other ways. He may already be a highly independent learner, especially about what interests him. He may be way ahead of his peers in his ability to access information via computer and the internet, and may be able to use his excellent memory to retain this information: even if no-one else knows, he knows it!

It is essential that the pupil with AS is given all the support possible to build on independent learning skills. These strengths will go with her into adulthood, and may well form the basis for successful study or employment later on. One of the strengths of AS is often the ability to work alone, without the need for social input or support.

Tony Attwood has written an excellent paper on the issues of homework and independent study. I suggest that you visit the website www.tonyattwood.com to read it (*Should Children with Autistic Spectrum Disorder be Exempt From Doing Homework?*), and draw it to the attention of the child's parent and discuss it with them if possible. Luke Jackson (a teenager with AS) provides a very good explanation of homework from the point of view of the child with AS in his book *Freaks, Geeks and Asperger Syndrome*. It is well worth a read and will help you understand your student's way of viewing the world (see the Further Reading section).

Chapter 7

How Do I Help with the Child's Stress?

It is amazing how quickly and totally things can go wrong for the pupil with AS. Usually this apparently sudden crisis can be prevented by the early spotting of potential difficulties. We need to stay 'on the ball' and to defuse situations before they overwhelm.

This chapter includes some techniques for defusing a child's stress early. They will help prevent the pupil reaching the point where their stress turns into undesirable behaviours. The last thing we want to do is only address their stress when they begin to shout, yell or lash out. Waiting for this to occur only teaches the child that it is necessary to act this way to get adult intervention.

So what should we do when things do go wrong? We may berate ourselves that we should have spotted it earlier, but that isn't going to help with the current crisis now! This chapter also includes strategies for working with a child who is already in a highly stressed state.

Manage your own emotions

Always remember that your response will have a direct influence on any tense situation. If you get angry as well, it will be like throwing petrol on a fire. If you stay calm and speak in a quiet voice, you will be a soothing influence. It doesn't matter how you feel inside, what matters is how you appear. Try and sort out conflicts when you are both calm. Children can't respond well when stressed either.

Allow a stress ball

A stress ball allows the child to squeeze and squash the tension out on the ball. The repetitive squeezing action can also be a calming movement for some children. Koosh balls and other fiddle toys may also help. Some children will find tremendous stress relief in reading and re-reading familiar books. Find out from the child what works for him.

Teach anger management

The following methods can be taught to your whole class but will particularly benefit the child with AS:

- Talk through the physical and emotional cues that let us know we are getting angry.

- Stop, Think, Do – Talk the class through this technique to use when getting angry. *Stop* what you are doing, *think* about what you could do and what might happen, choose the option that will keep you safe and *do* it.

- Teach pupils how, when they begin to get angry, to stop and slowly count to ten.

- Teach deep breathing techniques.

- Give safe alternatives to hitting – if there is a need to destroy, make it productive. Pupils can crush cans for recycling, tear up cardboard boxes so they can be laid flat for the recycling bin, etc.

Introduce Angry Cards

Like the Exit Card (see p.42), the Angry Card can be used when communication breaks down due to overload. The Angry Card replaces an outburst. It signals that the pupil feels that there has been an injustice (like giving the recipient a red card on the football field), but it replaces the need to rant or hit out. Matters provoking an Angry Card are dealt with later, after the situation has calmed down. At the time, the Angry Card is just a way of registering that the pupil is upset and providing an 'out' from the immediate situation.

Angry Cards only work if teachers always take them seriously and always act on them. Encourage the pupil with AS to issue the card to the teacher in charge, rather than to a fellow student. Therefore, if pupil A is angering pupil B by teasing him, pupil B gives the Angry Card to the teacher who then allows him some time out, perhaps in the safe haven, before finding some time later to sort out the issue. Additionally, the pupil is rewarded for using the Angry Card rather than lashing out.

Use the safe haven

Designate somewhere as a safe area the child can go to if stressed (see p.43). Make sure it is nearby and actually is safe. If it can't be out of the class then consider using a bean bag or the reading corner. Create some rules for its use regarding the time that can be spent in it. If the child is able to, she should let you know that she is going there or use an Exit Card (see p.42). It may be helpful to schedule a regular time for her to visit this place so that she can rest and recharge her batteries. Children with AS need this time out from the stress of dealing with busy classrooms. It may be that the safe haven is also a useful alternative to the busy yard at lunch and break times.

Deep pressure therapy

This needs to be discussed with the parents to see whether it works for their child and whether it is appropriate to do it at school. The most common use of it in the classroom is a weighted vest which helps keep some children calm. This can be put on as needed. Alternatively, a child who feels overwhelmed with tension may be helped by pushing against a wall or other strong structure, the feedback from the muscle strain providing relief for some children.

Security item

Talk with the parents or with the pupil herself about a particular item she finds comforting. For some children it is a piece of cloth that they like to touch, some like something with a particular smell (can also be used to block smells they find hard to cope with), for others it will be something to do with their special interest. The child can carry this with him and use it when he is stressed. However, be aware of the potential for bullying this strategy brings with it. The security item may open the child to ridicule, and the more unscrupulous fellow student may realize the trouble-making potential of stealing it. It may be better to keep security items with other possessions in the safe haven or Quiet Room.

Suggest burning-off anxiety

When the anxiety is at a low level, lots of these soothing techniques will be effective. When it is at a high level the child may need to burn it off. This can be done by going for a run or doing some other high energy exercise. Even taking a massage might help – although remember that, for some, massage is an unpleasant, even hurtful, experience. Some children with AS respond extremely well to physical activity as a form of stress relief. A quick run round the yard can be enough to settle the child and allow concentration to return.

Divert attention

If the child starts to get stressed and begins repeating things or gets stuck doing a routine, gently divert her attention to help her save face. Don't get drawn into answering repeated questions over and over. If necessary, suggest she diverts to her 'fall-back activity'(see p.41) and only return to the issue that was causing anxiety after she has been able to regain calm (and accessed support).

Use special interest as calmer

The most likely source of calm for the pupil with AS is his special interest. This is what he has created for himself as a secure place for his thoughts, and it is the subject his thoughts are most likely to return to if other things overwhelm him. Use his special interest and in this way go with, rather than against, his autism. If he needs five minutes drawing robots or looking through a book on mushrooms, allowing him to do so shows respect for his autism and allows him to manage a stressful situation for himself. You may do well to have a timer on hand, though, and agree a time limit if you are to have any chance of getting him back into your lesson after he has calmed down!

Provide a notebook of things not understood

Get the child to carry a notebook with him. In it he can jot down anything that he doesn't understand. These can be academic issues, social issues or anything of concern. Once a day he can share the notebook with you. It may be that this technique expands so that his parents and other teachers can jot down issues too.

Give text access to special needs advisor or other

If the child has a mobile phone, grant a mobile number that he can use to get help from the special needs advisor or another supportive adult. Make sure that the child has special permission (in writing) to use his phone in this way. A quick text could sort out a problem before it even starts to develop, and a quick check, for example, that a room change means that the next lesson really is in Lab.3, can prevent all sorts of anxieties building up and blocking other learning.

Provide regular check-ins

It can be useful to schedule a certain time each day when you and the pupil can chat about things and monitor overall progress. With the older student, this check-in could be with the special needs advisor or with her form tutor. It provides a good opportunity to explain things that are confusing the child or what she is worrying about. A simple distracting activity often eases the pressure of talking in these situations (e.g. colouring-in for the younger child, or helping with an activity such as photocopying for the older). This proactive checking can ensure that you are not using the pupil's behaviour as a benchmark as to how well she is doing. The quiet and compliant child with AS may be struggling just as much as the one with violent outbursts, but may just be a lot less visible.

Keep consequences relevant

When a child with AS does something that is really inappropriate, the consequence must be relevant to what has happened and involve *doing* something rather than just words. Saying sorry may have very little meaning. If she has taken something belonging to someone else then maybe she should share something of hers. When something has happened, always look back and work out what the precipitant (cause) was. This will help you work out the appropriate consequence. Have a discussion with the child after she has calmed down, about inappropriate and unacceptable behaviours. Use diagrams or other visual aids. Make sure you deal with the underlying issue as well as whatever inappropriate action that drew your attention to it.

Agree together what is 'fair', since the concept can be very important to many people with AS and a consequence that feels unfair is likely to do far more harm than good.

Pick your battle

Work on those behaviours that are unacceptable. The child will probably have other behaviours that many will label as odd – don't worry about these if they are not having a negative consequence. Choose the battles you need to win and respect the difference in the child's other behaviour. One of your jobs as a teacher is to model acceptance, and accepting difference and even celebrating unusualness can have a great knock-on effect with the other members of the school.

Allow reasonable differentiation

It is not the responsibility of the child with AS to fit into school at all costs. We want pupils to be proud of having AS and the strengths that it gives them. It is OK to allow the pupil with AS in your class to behave rather differently, to avoid certain activities or to do different work. Inclusion means making sure that the child's differences are accommodated, so be brave about standing up for the child with AS's right to be different!

Consider reward systems

All children respond strongly to reward systems and they can be particularly effective for children with AS who have such a keen sense of fairness and a very strong need to achieve. However, systems based on intrinsic rewards have much less effect on children with AS than they do on other children. Therefore, when designing the reward system, try to set it up so that the child is earning something tangible. Introduce intangible/social rewards alongside so he starts to develop a liking for them. Usually it is best to reward a little often rather than a lot occasionally, and beware of over-rewarding as encouragement. If the child receives a 'merit' for remembering all his books and equipment one week he may feel it very unfair if he does not receive another for doing the same the next!

Adapt the sensory environment

It is important to remain aware of how much the sensory environment may be contributing to the stress of a pupil with AS. Try to adapt the sensory environment to prevent stress rather than merely dealing with it when it occurs.

Auditory

A child's behaviour can be altered by a noise that others, including yourself, do not notice. Tantrums might occur at the same time of day and be linked, for example, back to the caretaker raking leaves. Here are some strategies for dealing with this sensitivity:

- Identify and eliminate, where possible, high pitched continuous noises (e.g. electric motors), and sharp, startling noises. If you are unable to do this, seat the child away from the source of such noises.

- Have a quiet place the child can go and work.

- Let the child wear earplugs to block out distracting background noise.

- Let the child listen to soothing music using an iPod or similar. The music needs to be carefully chosen. Some students benefit from hearing 'white noise', which seems to blot out distractions.

Visual

Some children with AS can be particularly sensitive to light, especially bright, flickering or some forms of artificial light. This can make it difficult or even painful for them to concentrate. If this is the case:

- Seat the child where he is not in direct sunlight.

- Avoid fluorescent bulbs where possible. Otherwise, provide a lamp with a standard bulb on his desk.

- Let the child wear sunglasses.

- Get him to cup his hands around his eyes to block peripheral vision if he is becoming overwhelmed.

Tactile

Children with AS often have tactile sensitivities quite unlike those of other children.

- Clothes are often a real issue for children with AS. Talk with the parents to ensure the child is wearing clothes that she is comfortable in.

- Modify uniform requirements. Perhaps he could wear a soft school sports fleece rather than a collar and tie, or a soft undershirt under his formal shirt.

- It is often useful if the clothes are easy to put on and take off, especially if the child has difficulty with fine motor skills. Make sure that the child can cope with changes of clothing required during the school day.

- Learn where the sensitive areas of the body are for the child you are teaching. It may be that a touch might really hurt her even (or for some children, especially) if she is only touched lightly. Allow her to move out of the line, or to avoid crossing a busy hall if there is a danger of her being jostled.

- Remember that the child may have a very high pain threshold. Try a verbal check-list ('Does your throat hurt? Do you have a pain in your head?' etc.). You often need to look for behavioural signs that show she may be in pain, such as increased irritability or sudden un-cooperativeness. If these happen, notify parents so they can be on the lookout for ear infections or similar.

Olfactory

Children with AS are often hypersensitive to smell. They can often smell things that other children can't smell, and may find some smells unbearable. You can help to prevent problems with this in the following ways:

- Avoid wearing strong perfumes or aftershaves.

- Allow fresh air to circulate in the class.

- Be aware that anything strong smelling in a class may create a difficulty for a child with AS.

- Allow her to bring to class a small item impregnated with a calming smell.

- Be aware that she may actually be comforted by her own smell. You need to intervene if she is allowing personal hygiene to lapse as this is not going to help her social acceptance.

Taste

Children with AS are sensitive to both the taste and the texture of food, and tend to be wary of new things and resistant to change. They are often creatures of habit where food is concerned and often prefer to eat the same thing day after day.

If your school provides lunches:

- Send school lunch menus home in advance so that she can choose without pressure.

- Allow her first entry into the dining hall so that there is a full choice of food and the room is not 'messy' with previous people's food.

- Allow a quiet area for lunch. Do not expect her to socialize and eat.

- Allow the pupil to bring a packed lunch and don't worry if it is always exactly the same (although you could discuss with parents if it really is nutritionally unsuitable).

- Do not push the issue of food. Be aware of the danger of eating disorders developing as the child grows up. Keep issues of food relaxed and non-confrontational.

School environments and sensory difficulties

Within any environment there are a large number of stimuli. When introducing a child with AS into a new environment, think about the stimuli and decide whether the child will be able to tolerate them. Let him watch the first time and then join in.

School assemblies are a prime example. The crowdedness, action at the front, smell of bodies and intense noise can absolutely overwhelm some children. Often it is better that he has some quiet time during assemblies rather than forcing him into what is a torturous situation. For other children it may be the music rooms or technology laboratory that prove to be too much. See whether there is a less stressful alternative available (see Chapter 12).

Chapter 8

What Should the Teacher Aide be Focusing on?

Ideally you will be able to secure some teacher aide time for the child. Explore as many avenues for funding as you can. The teacher aide should always be working to help the child become more independent and be teaching her coping strategies, rather than becoming someone the child relies on and who rescues her. If that is kept in mind, then the teacher aide will always be beneficial. In brief, things they could do include:

- Showing the child how to get her things organized for the day.

- Helping the child invent a system for keeping her possessions organized.

- Encouraging the child to be sociable, flexible and co-operative in various situations.

- Spotting ways of using the child's special interest to motivate her to do class work.

- Helping her understand the unwritten rules of social interaction by using comic strip conversations or discussing situations with the child explaining what other people may be thinking, or what leads them to do certain things.

- Writing social stories to aid the child's understanding of feelings and friendships (may need training to do this effectively).

- Encouraging her to talk with others. Be the prompt that whispers in her ear suggestions of what to say.

- Doing exercises prescribed by professional support people to improve motor skills.

- Giving extra tuition in areas of difficulty.

- Showing the child ways of dealing with sensory sensitivity.

Where possible get the teacher aide to work with the child both individually and as part of a group made up of a cross-section of the class. This is important for the child's self-esteem.

In addition, the teacher aide can be invaluable in creating and introducing strategies that develop social skills, self-organization and techniques for making sense of the world. There are many of these, often created by autism experts. Many of these strategies are extremely useful for a person with AS, but they take time to implement and manage, time that is not always available to the class teacher.

Some of the strategies that are easiest to implement are given here. If you or the teacher aide have success with these, I strongly encourage you to extend them by attending some specialist training.

Where they require tools to be made, ideally they will be created and managed by a teacher aide, but will be available to everyone, including other teachers, the parents and essentially the pupil himself. If effective they can form techniques that can be adapted and carried forward into adult life.

Create a visual organiser

The ability of children with AS to think in pictures can be used to aid their organization. A common strategy for younger children is to use visual organizers in the form of a series of pictures or symbols showing the sequence of events or tasks to be done. It is important to remember just how useful this strategy can be, if adapted slightly, for the older pupil too. It is also important to be aware of how much time it takes to implement these strategies successfully. The pupil with AS will need to learn to use it gradually, and his level of use will change constantly as he grows up. A teacher aide can be ideally placed to work on the long-term development of this support strategy.

When creating a visual organizer, first ask yourself what you wish to achieve with it. You may wish to create one that shows the sequences of subjects or events over the whole school day, or perhaps over just one lesson. You may just wish to break down the tasks that the child needs to do during draft writing, or reading.

Next discuss with the teacher aide the physical form the organizer will take. If the child does not like to be singled out, then you may want to create a large organizer that can be used with the whole class. If the child needs more assistance, a personal one that can fit on the top of her desk may be more useful. A general organizer can be physical (where the pictures are actually placed onto a board in sequence) or virtual (where a computer or whiteboard is used to indicate the sequence of events). In either case, any changes to the order need be carefully explained before the tasks are swapped around.

The next step is to create the images that will represent each task or event. Some children may find abstract pictures hard to interpret so photographs of the actual objects may work better. For example, if you are doing an organizer for the whole day, you may have a photograph of a reading book for reading time or a photograph of the computer for information technology. For some children a drawing of a book or a computer may be sufficient. Colour often helps and you should write the word that matches the picture underneath it, for example, 'Reading' under the picture of the book. In time, the organizer becomes entirely word-based and becomes a conventional plan for the day.

For the older student (or adult) the visual organizer becomes a timetable or diary. A hand-held computer device such as a smartphone, iPad or other tablet device, can provide the ideal visual support for the sequence of events through an activity or throughout a day. Changes in plans can be emailed or altered on the daily calendar function. In this way, a skill developed as a coping strategy when very young can be adapted and developed to provide independent support right into adulthood.

Arguably, examples such as these are some of the most useful learning that can be provided during the school years for the pupil with AS.

Help the child with social skills

There are plenty of things that can be done to assist with the development of social skills for the child with AS. Make sure that whatever is being done in school complements things done by any other professionals working with the child and with work done by the parents. Talk with the parents to make sure there is consistency, and include them in discussions and planning. This is an ideal opportunity both to provide parental support, and to allow the parents the opportunity to contribute to the social programme their children will follow in school.

Social stories™

One of the tools recognized as most effective for helping to explain and develop understanding of social situations is a social story. These can be used by anyone working with the child, but are perhaps a particularly good strategy for the teacher aide to introduce.

A social story is a technique developed by Carol Gray to help children understand social situations. If you are keen to try these I suggest you read the literature available on them (see the References section at the end of this book). In brief they consist of four types of sentences:

- *Descriptive* – tells us who is involved, what she is doing and where she is.

- *Perspective* – explains the reactions and feelings of the others involved.

- *Directive* – tells the child what she needs to do or say.

- *Control* – gives the child a way of remembering what to do or say.

There should be a ratio of around five descriptive sentences for every one directive sentence. When writing the stories you have to be very accurate – use words like 'usually', 'sometimes' and 'often' so as not to make the situation too rigid. In the directive sentences avoid words like 'must' and 'will'. Use phrases like 'will try to'. Here is an example of a social story:

> One of the rooms at school is my classroom (descriptive). The one that is mine at the moment is known as room 8 (descriptive). The same children usually work in room 8 each day (descriptive). A bell rings early in the morning (descriptive). The children know that when the bell rings they have to go to their classroom (perspective). We have to go to our room so that the teacher can help us learn (perspective). When I hear the first bell I will try to go straight to my classroom (directive). Children go straight to classrooms like trains go straight to their stations (control). My teacher will be pleased that I have gone straight to my classroom (perspective).

Comic strip conversations

These are used to illustrate how communication works. They consist of stick figure drawings, simple symbols and colour coding. Pictures are drawn to show a sequence of events. By breaking down a conversation (either actual or hypothetical) and using visual cues, a child can see what is happening, bit by bit.

If you are interested in asking your teaching aide to try this technique, it can be useful if both of you read the relevant literature so that you have an understanding of the common symbols and conventions that have been proven to be most effective (see References section).

Friendship circles

The teacher aide could use this pencil and paper technique to explain the different levels of friendship. Start with a small circle with the child's name in. Add a circle around it and put the names of close family members in the circle. Then add another circle around it with the next level of family or friends. You can write between the circles the appropriate way to interact with the various people.

For example, a friendship circle was created for a boy called Jack, who has been greeting strangers with a kiss and a hug as he does with close family. His name was placed in the centre. The next circle contained the names of those closest to him. In the bubble was an explanation of how he is to interact with these people. The next circle out was the next closest group of people to him and an explanation of how to interact with them, etc. What is placed in the bubbles will be dependent on the child, as will the number of circles and whose names appear in them.

Role play

Ask the teacher aide to go back over situations the student found difficult or stressful using role play. She should pause as she goes to explain people's thoughts and feelings at various stages.

Openers and closers

Perhaps the teacher aide could help by teaching the child phrases he can use to start conversation and play, and phrases he can use to end it. Get him to practise with her and with you. Some phrases to use if he is invited to play but doesn't wish to join in would also be useful. He should be taught that pauses in a conversation signal the right time to start speaking.

Interest clubs

A teacher aide may be able to set up interest clubs, particularly around the pupil's special interests. These provide a great opportunity for the child to be included and given status by peers. They also provide structured and safely supervised activities as an alternative to the unstructured and often rather hazardous times of break and lunch.

Buddies

The rest of the class can be an invaluable support to the child with AS if managed correctly. Remember that you, as the teacher, must model how to respectfully interact with the child. Carefully choose people to be buddies in difficult situations. This can take the form of buddies who work with the child at certain times of the day, buddies to help them in the playground or buddies for them to go to if they are feeling stressed out. Take the time to talk over with the buddies exactly what you expect of them. Explain why it is that the child needs their support and that they are being trusted with a very important task. Let them know that they can come and see you any time if they don't know what to do.

It can be a good idea to nominate teacher aide time to check-in regularly with the buddies to see how often the child is making use of them and if they need any help. Always reward the buddies for their good work.

Watching for cues

Other children provide cues as to how to act in any given situation. A teacher aide who can work alongside the child with AS is ideally placed to watch with him and to point out how to take cues from others. Eventually he will be able to use this skill throughout life to help judge what behaviour is appropriate.

When first starting out, she should explain how you can look at others to see how they are acting. For example, are they silent, talking quietly or running around? She could point out children in the class who are good role models that he can look at to see how he should be acting. These children should also be made aware that they will be helping, particularly as they may get stared at intensely for the first few days!

Discuss why you are choosing these particular children. Tell the child with AS that some children know the best way to behave more than others. A child with AS can easily be led astray, so this step is very important.

TV programmes

This activity is more easily done at home, and is one you could encourage parents to get involved with. It also provides an ideal one-to-one activity for the teacher aide to undertake with the pupil, perhaps during a session when you have agreed it is better for the child to withdraw from class.

Pre-record TV programmes such as *3rd Rock from the Sun* and *Mr Bean*, where characters act in a different manner from what is generally acceptable. Explain that you will be watching a fun programme where characters do funny things. Watch a segment of the programme with the child. Watch it again but this time pause the programme when the characters do something that is inappropriate. Talk about what is inappropriate and discuss what they could have done instead.

Be careful that this activity does not make the child more self-conscious. Keep the session light-hearted and have a laugh at the silly things that are done.

Prompts

If the child is going to be required to talk to someone he is unfamiliar with (e.g. a student teacher, visiting researcher), the teacher aide can stand beside the child and whisper suggestions of what to say in the child's ear.

Help the child in the playground

Extra support during the unstructured times of break and lunch can be one of the most essential activities that a teacher aide can provide. The playground is probably the most threatening environment you could put a child with AS into. Vast open spaces, complex social interactions, a myriad of unwritten rules to adhere to and a plethora of sounds, sights and smells combine to make a child with AS feel at a loss. It is also a situation in which a child with AS who has poor motor skills will stand out like a sore thumb and be particularly vulnerable to bullying, both physical and verbal. This does not get any easier as he becomes older, as the social rules of non-teaching time become, if anything, even more complex as you grow up.

Many of the skills discussed so far will aid the child in coping in the playground environment. In addition, here are a few more tips:

- Have places where the child can go if it all becomes too much. Allow access to the safe haven and ensure that it is supervised.

- Identify who the child can go to for help if she needs it.

- Encourage any positive friendships you see developing.

- Encourage Craze of the Week and other formal/ structured activities, ideally monitored by teaching aides.

- Establish homework or other special interest clubs.

- Consider arranging for the child a mix of the first half of lunch in the playground and the second half in a quiet place (e.g. library). This will help the child relax and prepare herself for the afternoon's work.

- Make sure other staff are properly informed about AS and the implications for the child so they can keep an eye on things (see Chapter 10).

- Talk to the child about the difference between teasing and joking. What cues are there that a person is doing one or the other? Teach her how to respond appropriately.

Using the teacher aide in the playground rather than solely in the classroom is extremely important. She can help the child make sense of it all and coach him through social situations. Discuss the importance of the role with her, so she does not feel she is being used as a 'Dinner Nanny' or minder, without sufficient professional involvement. Make sure, too, that she gets a break before she has to return to the classroom.

Exploring emotions

Once a week, ask the teacher aide to prepare some material on studying an emotion. Brainstorm when the emotion occurs, what the cues are, how people act and some phrases to use to express this emotion. This is an activity that can be beneficial to the whole class. The child may actually learn more from other children's answers. Spending some time one-on-one with the child afterwards, recapping what is discussed, will help to reinforce the learning.

Topic talking times

Often other children do not wish to hear about the child's special interest every day. It can help to tell the child to avoid talking about the special topic in class or in the playground and instead set up a particular time when he can talk about this topic with the teacher aide. Ultimately, it can help to teach the child the signs to watch out for that indicate when a person has heard enough. This can be particularly difficult, as a child will often forget about everything else as he starts to talk about his special interest…and he may not particularly care if the listener is bored or not anyway!

Be alert to bullying

Having an extra adult to help keep an eye on the pupil with AS can be a great help in spotting bullying early, and implementing the strategies covered in this chapter will all help children with AS to avoid becoming a victim of bullying. Unfortunately their lack of social understanding and motor skills makes them very visible. Combine this with their inability to understand someone else's motivations and you have a prime target for bullying. Is there anything else you can do? Bullying is often drastically reduced if the child is not isolated in the playground. Therefore the buddy system discussed earlier in the chapter will help out here. A person that is keeping an eye out for them or someone they can go for help will assist greatly. However, there is no substitute for real friends and although a buddy may develop into a friend, this does not happen automatically. What we need to do is help friendships to form.

To do this, many people make the mistake of finding another child with AS, putting the two of them together and calling them friends. In fact in this situation they are even less likely to become friends, as neither knows quite what they are supposed to do. Just think how you would react if you were placed with another person just because they have the same hair colour as you and were told that you should be friends! A far more successful method is to use interest clubs or to foster any small friendships you see naturally forming. Friendship is usually based upon shared interests so you are going to have the most success if you spot the child interacting with another child with similar interests and encourage the two to do something together based upon those interests.

Make sure that it is not the case that the responsibility for keeping the pupil with AS safe falls onto the shoulders of teacher aides alone. All staff in the school need to be made aware of the child's identity and vulnerability (see Chapter 10). This is because it is hard to spot the most common form of bullying a child with AS will be subjected to – getting the child to unwittingly do something they shouldn't. Other children will soon learn that they can tell the child with AS to do or say things and that child will happily go and do or say them. Other children only need to pretend that they are being friendly and the child with AS will take what they say to be completely true. At the other children's suggestion the child with AS will then unwittingly go along and break school rules or act inappropriately. A teacher will spot this and the child will be in trouble and be completely confused as to why. Staff need to be trained to look beyond what they see the child with AS doing, to what caused them to do it and deal with that aspect firmly.

Chapter 9

Who Else in the School Needs to Know?

This is a sensitive issue that needs to be discussed with the parents and, ultimately, with the pupil himself. Is he aware of his own diagnosis? If not, although it may not be your place to tell him, you will need to support the parents (perhaps with the help of health professionals) to do so. He has a right to be aware of his own condition, and it will be very difficult to grant him the support and differentiation he deserves (and is entitled to in law) if he is not aware of his own diagnosis. When he should be told may depend on his age and level of development, although if the disclosure is made in a positive way there is no real reason to delay. There is nothing wrong with having AS!

It is essential that all staff in school have a good understanding of AS so they do not misinterpret the child's actions and can be ready to differentiate as appropriate. They need to be aware of the possibility of AS, even if disclosure of an individual child's diagnosis is not made. If they do not have this understanding and so do not allow reasonable differentiation they could unintentionally be causing the child harm. Staff need to be aware of this and aware of how their behaviour is likely to impact on the pupil with AS.

People react in different ways to being told someone has a condition like AS. Ill-informed staff may fall into any number of mistakes:

- Putting the diagnosis down to an excuse for poor behaviour using the latest psychobabble.

- Using the diagnosis as an excuse to exclude the child from activities rather than finding ways to include her.

- Confusing the diagnosis with other conditions.

- Spreading the news around and discussing it openly without regard for the child or her family's preference on disclosure.

- Refusing to believe the diagnosis and insisting the pupil takes part in activities she finds distressing.

Good AS training needs to be made available to all staff so that they do not risk falling into these errors. It is important that AS awareness extends to non-teaching staff as well as teaching, as these staff are often 'in charge' during the most vulnerable periods (on the bus, during lunch) in the pupil with AS's day.

It is still possible to provide reasonable adjustment for the pupil with AS even if he does not yet know about his condition or if he prefers not to disclose it. If this is the case you may have to work more covertly.

You could arrange a time to talk with the class about different learning styles. Discuss how some people like to work in lots of noise and some with none, how some like skipping through books quickly and some like reading from start to finish, and how some people like things to change and be different all the time and some like things always to remain the same. Even young children seem to grasp this concept well.

You could create a chart with all the different ways people like to learn and all the different learning environments that people find helpful. With older children you can get them to identify what they think works best for them and display these on a wall. This will help the children in the class be more tolerant of each other and provides you with a way of relating AS to the class.

After completing this exercise you can explain that you are using certain strategies with the individual pupil because of his unique learning style, which of course is true! He will be able to relate to this and will already know that everyone has unique learning styles – not just him. Children that know they have AS can also benefit from looking at it in this manner, particularly if they are self-conscious about having AS.

You will most likely find, however, that most pupils are comfortable with their diagnosis, especially if the school ethos towards difference is a positive one. Many individuals have always known they are different and experience relief more than anything at finding out it is due to having AS. As diagnosis gets better and swifter, many people are aware of their AS from a very early age, and many are extremely proud of their unusual and very valuable characteristics. The confident pupil with AS may well be the very best person to give a presentation on AS, on its advantages and blessings just as much as on its drawbacks.

Reading a children's book on AS can also be helpful. A good one is *Blue Bottle Mystery* (and its sequels) by Kathy Hoopman (see References section). For older children, Luke Jackson's books provide a useful perspective from the teenager's point of view and the now classic *The Curious Incident of the Dog in the Night-Time* by Mark Haddon can be an excellent reader to study in class. Emphasizing that Isaac Newton, Albert Einstein, Vincent Van Gogh, Leonardo Da Vinci, Beethoven...any number of famous people are likely to have had AS will help, too, in establishing that there is more to the condition than simply a 'disability'.

Chapter 10

What Should Happen before the Child Changes Class or School?

Children with AS resist change in most aspects of their lives as they find it incredibly stressful. A change of class, therefore, and even more so a change of school, are going to be especially stressful due to the scale of change. If you can do the following, you will ease the transition.

- Give the pupil plenty of warning about the change in school and work with the parents on making the change open and transparent. Encourage the parents to make these decisions as early as possible.

- Get the new teacher or school special needs advisor to come and observe your classroom. She can pick up on strategies and routines that are working well in your class.

- If possible make sure new teachers meet the child with AS more than once before the necessary transition.

- Arrange for a 'Key Contact' so that parents and pupils have someone they can go to for information about the new school. Make sure that this person has a full understanding of the child with AS, so that she can disseminate information as needed.

- Spend some time working with the pupil with AS, writing down all the ways she has managed her AS successfully in her current school. It is important that all these successful strategies are not lost.

- Make yourself available as a resource person for the new teachers. Pass on tips and tricks.

- Organize for the child to visit the new class or school a number of times. Point out major landmarks that she can use to orientate herself. Allow her to take photographs so that she can go back over what she has seen later.

- Have lots of these visits and schedule them for different times of the day so the pupil can see different things happening.

- Collect paraphernalia associated with the new school (planner, map, swipe card, library card, etc.) so that the pupil can become familiar with it all.

- Check levels of AS understanding at the new school. This could be a perfect opportunity for them to have some AS top-up training.

- See whether you can arrange a period of overlap with the existing and new support staff so everyone has time to learn and adjust.

- Make sure that arrangements for leaving the current school (including any farewell events, end of term parties, etc.) are well handled. Changes of routine at the end of school may upset the pupil with AS, and you don't want her leaving her old school with negative feelings.

Transition for the pupil with AS is a huge subject. There have been some very useful books written on the subject recently, particularly *Successful School Change and Transition for the Child with Asperger Syndrome* by Clare Lawrence (see Further Reading section) and a workbook to use with the pupil with AS, *Making The Move* by K. I. Al-Ghani and Lynda Kenward (see Further Reading section for details).

Chapter 11

How Can the Wider School Help?

Because this is a book for teachers most of it is very practical and immediate. However, some issues need a whole school approach to make everyone's life easier, and these are given here for discussion with head teachers, special needs advisors or other policy makers.

Arrange an alternative PE programme

Due to their poor motor skills and difficulty with social interaction, team sports are a huge challenge for children with AS. Working on one of these two skills is very taxing for the child and working on both at once can be almost impossible. PE then becomes a time of great stress for both the child and the teacher and often very little is achieved. It is usually far more beneficial for the child to do an alternative PE programme when you are doing team sports with the class. A rotation of responsible classmates can be trained in two-person PE games that help with motor skills and coordination. Most people would perceive there to be a stigma associated with being separated from the class like this but for the child with AS it is usually a great relief and far better than the alternative. Where it is not possible to 'rescue' the child with AS in this way and for some reason he needs to be included in team sports, make sure that the teams are selected by the teacher, not by the children in the class. Alternatively, allow him to go to the safe haven or Quiet Room and study instead. Taking part in PE is not really essential, but maintaining the child's well-being and self-esteem most definitely are. Physical fitness can be addressed in other ways. Many families are using interactive gaming consoles, for example!

Home and school communication

Consistency is key for children with AS. It is really important that everyone involved with the child works hard to keep the flow of communication open. This is particularly important between home and school. As the child gets older, there will be more and more occasions where they are moving between teachers and everyone needs to be on the same page.

- The school website needs to be kept updated, and could have a section specifically highlighting changes for the coming day or week. Any changes in teacher or room could be given here as soon as they are known in the staffroom. Electronic notice boards are another good way of keeping information available.

- Most schools now use an email system. This is invaluable in allowing the pupil with AS to check details of homework or class activity, and as a quick and efficient communication tool between the student and a member of staff appointed to give this support. Texts work well too.

- The school could establish a before-school 'chat room', open to any students invited to join by the special needs advisor. This could be a venue for checking details of the day that are worrying the pupil, as well as providing some online social interaction. Could this social support be extended to include the real world at break time or lunch?

Quiet Room

One of the most essential pieces of support for the pupil with AS, as mentioned many times in this book, is the safe haven or Quiet Room. Space is often at a premium in schools, and it may take some persuasive argument to get the policymakers to agree that a space be set aside in this way. Keep arguing! The pupil with AS needs this sanctuary if he is to cope with the hustle and noise, with the confusion and the inconsistency of the rest of the school community.

Subject choices

The school principal or head teacher may need to get involved, and may even have to take on the regional education policymakers, in order to win the right for the pupil with AS to follow a different education programme.

Perhaps the official policy is that all students need to study a modern foreign language. Yet is that really going to benefit a student with AS who is struggling to communicate in his home tongue? Perhaps the policy is that all students study an hour of class music a week. If this time is deeply uncomfortable for the student with AS, is he really benefiting from that time? Make sure that a reduced timetable is never used as an excuse for excluding the pupil with AS from something he wants to do or could do profitably, and make sure that communication is kept open on these policies between all staff, the health professionals involved, the parents and of course the child himself. That said, make sure that the child's time is spent usefully at school, even if that means him following a slightly different programme of study to his peers. He is different – he has AS – and recognition of that difference can often be the most respectful solution to many problems.

Asperger community

Most schools will have more than one student with AS. If the prevalence in society for autism spectrum disorders overall is something like 1:100, a larger school may well have several students with AS. Given this, is there an opportunity here to allow an Asperger community to form? AS is in many ways a separate culture, made up of people who view the world rather differently and have different priorities, challenges and interests. Perhaps the older student with AS would be the ideal person to help the younger one with his homework. Perhaps the parents of a pupil who has had a diagnosis for many years would be ideally placed to offer support and advice to parents new to the diagnosis. The head teacher or special needs advisor are ideally placed to facilitate links of this kind. All that is needed is the mind set to bring AS 'out of the closet' and allow these natural support structures to form.

Lunch

It may have to be a whole-school decision to allow the pupil with AS to miss lunch, to bring a packed lunch, to go home for lunch or to eat lunch in a different room. Many teachers may feel they are making too much of the issue to request this level of differentiation, but if the pupil is so distressed by the current lunchtime arrangements that she is incapable of learning in the afternoons, then something fairly radical needs to be done.

Exams

If your student is going to do as well as she can in exams, to properly reflect the learning that has taken place in the years you have spent with her, there needs to be differentiation in exams. She may need a scribe to write for her, access to a computer, a separate room, an altered exam timetable... Even if you are teaching the child during her early years you may still feel that it is important to raise these issues. The sooner the understanding of her needs can be established the better.

Liaison with health professionals

It is surprising just how difficult it still is in some places for health professionals to gain free access to schools. Health professionals are not teachers and do not necessarily understand how schools work. If the support they are going to suggest for the child, and the advice they give to the parents, is going to work in the real world of your classroom then they need free access to come in and learn what that world really entails. It may need a school policy decision to really open up this access, and will need a level of professional trust on both sides.

Counsellor support

Many schools offer a school nurse or counsellor who can be accessed to give advice to young people. This may be advice on stress, on school work or managing homework demands, on friendship and relationship problems, sexual health and safety, drugs, alcohol or any other issues that concern young people these days. It is imperative that the young person with AS has access to someone who has an understanding of AS. Not only will the very fact of having AS throw up all sorts of problems not necessarily met by the neuro-typical young person, but having AS will also mean a rather different viewpoint on all the usual young people's issues too. Could the school provide an autism or AS-aware expert to provide specific counselling and advice? Could this be delivered to the 'Asperger community' mentioned above, as a separate group? Could the school provide an AS helpline or drop-in time? If you are at a smaller school, could you band together with neighbouring schools and have someone visit all the schools one day each fortnight? What about the issue of wider staff awareness and training? Awareness of AS is a whole-school issue. As the teacher of pupils with AS you are well placed to raise the profile of the needs of the many and varied members of the school community that AS affects.

Chapter 12

Am I Qualified to Teach this Child?

Many teachers feel inadequate when faced with the task of teaching a pupil with AS. How can I do the best for her? Will my lack of training and AS knowledge mean that I'm letting her down?

The age and experience of the teacher, prior experience with AS and additional qualifications have only a small impact on the teacher's ability to teach a child with AS. What is far more important is that the teacher is calm, predictable and flexible. You as the teacher need to maintain a good sense of humour and be prepared to ask for help whenever you need it.

Remember that you have an expert in the needs of a pupil with AS available all the time in your classroom: the child himself. He will know what he finds difficult, what alarms and frightens him, what sensory issues are bothering him, what is confusing him and blocking understanding. Over time he will become more aware and able to articulate his feelings. Work with him and be prepared to learn from him.

Be forever looking for the positives in the child and ensure your classroom is a place of encouragement, not criticism. Model acceptance of the child's AS for the other pupils and encourage a view point that it's 'OK to be different'. Be prepared to celebrate the quirky and the original in what the child does and says.

Anyone can teach a child with AS, so long as they have the right attitude. Maintain your sense of humour and remember that so much of AS is fascinating, unusual and eye-opening. Hans Asperger himself said 'These children...can be guided and taught, but only by those who give them true understanding and genuine affection, people who show kindness towards them and yes, humour' (Asperger 1944, p.46). Enjoy sharing in the child's unique view of the world!

I Want to Know More – Where Should I Start?

I have listed the references I have used at the back of the book. The full reference for any book I mention in this section can be found in the References and/or Further Reading sections.

If I could recommend only two books that I have read at the time of publishing, they would have to be Tony Attwood's *Asperger's Syndrome: A Guide For Parents and Professionals* (1998) or his updated version, *The Complete Guide to Asperger Syndrome* (2007) and the *OASIS Guide to Asperger's Syndrome* (Kirby and Romanwski 2001). Tony Attwood's books have comprehensive information in easy-to-read language and the OASIS guide has large amounts of extra background information on a wide variety of areas to do with AS. Both these books are linked to excellent websites. Tony Attwood's site also contains the paper he wrote about homework. Both are wonderful springboards for finding more information.

If you are having specific issues with the child in your class then *Asperger Syndrome – Practical Strategies for the Classroom* by George Thomas, Phil Whitaker, Penny Barratt, Heather Clewley, Helen Joy and Mo Potter

(Leicester City Council and Leicestershire County Council) could be very useful. It is organized by areas of difficulty. You look up the specific section on what you or the child are having trouble with. Each section contains a brief example of the difficulty, some reasons it occurs and a couple of strategies that help with it. Another book, *How to Make School Make Sense* by Clare Lawrence is a great guide to how to help the child with AS to understand school.

The other type of book to explore is one written by someone with AS. *Pretending to be Normal* by Liane Holliday Willey, talks about what it has been like growing up with AS. *Asperger Syndrome, the Universe and Everything* by Kenneth Hall is an insightful little book written by a child coming to terms with AS. *Freaks, Geeks and Asperger Syndrome: A User Guide To Adolescence* by Luke Jackson is a witty and insightful book by a teenager with AS. He cleverly balances explaining his experiences of AS to the general reader with tips and pieces of wisdom for other teenagers with AS. For insight into the world as seen by children with AS and autism *The Hidden World of Autism* by Rebecca Chilvers is fascinating and very moving. To understand the struggle parents go through try *Eating an Artichoke* by Echo R Fling. In particular, it provides insights on the struggles with educational placement.

One of the best books on visual strategies that can be used in a classroom is *Visual Strategies for Improving Communication* by Linda A Hodgdon. It contains plenty of practical ideas with examples.

Most countries have Autism Associations that will be able to provide you with more specific information and support. A growing number also have organizations dedicated to AS.

Some contact details for these organizations follow.

Australia

Autism Spectrum Australia
Phone: +61 02 8977 8300
Post: Forest Ridge Business Park, Building 1, Level 2, Aquatic Drive, French Forest, NSW 2086
Website: www.aspect.org.au

Canada

Autism Society Canada
Phone: 1 866 476 8440 Or ++1 613 789 8943
Post: PO Box 22017, 1670 Heron Road, Ottawa, Ontario, K1V OC2
Email: info@autismsocietycanada.ca
Website: www.autismsocietycanada.ca

New Zealand

Autism New Zealand
Phone: 0800 AUTISM (288 476) +64 4 470 7616
Email: info@autismnz.org.nz (National Office)
Fax: +64 4 470 7617

And of course there is the **Cloud 9 Children's Foundation** in New Zealand who commissioned the writing of the first edition of this book:
Phone: + 64 4 232 4795
Post: PO Box 51176
TAWA 5249, Wellington, New Zealand
Email: foundation@entercloud9.com
Website: www.withyoueverystepoftheway.com

UK

National Autistic Society
Phone: ++44 20 7833 2299
Post: 393 City Road London EC1V 1NG UK
Email: nas@nas.org.uk
Website: www.nas.org.uk

USA

Autism Society of America
Phone: 1 800 3AUTISM Or ++1 301 657 0881
Post: 4340 East-West Hwy, Suite 350, Bethesda, Maryland 20814
USA
Email: membership@autism-society.org
Website: www.autism-society.org

Asperger Syndrome Coalition of the US
Phone: 1 866 4ASPRGR
Post: PO Box 351268 Jacksonville, FL 32235–1268
Email: info@aspergersyndrome.org
Website: www.asperger.org

I hope you have many enjoyable experiences teaching a child with AS and come to recognize the special gifts that they have.

Further Reading

Al-Ghani, K.I. and Kenward, L. (2009) *Making the Move: A Guide for Schools and Parents on the Transfer of Pupils with Autism Spectrum Disorders (ASDs) from Primary to Secondary School.* London: Jessica Kingsley Publishers.

Attwood, T. (1998) *Asperger's Syndrome: A Guide for Parents and Professionals.* London: Jessica Kingsley Publishers.

Attwood, T. (2007) *The Complete Guide to Asperger's Syndrome.* London: Jessica Kingsley Publishers.

Chilvers, R. (2007) *The Hidden World of Autism.* London: Jessica Kingsley Publishers.

Haddon, M. (2003) *The Curious Incident of the Dog in the Night-Time.* London: Jonathan Cape.

Jackson, L. (2002) *Freaks, Geeks and Asperger's Syndrome: A User Guide to Adolescence.* London: Jessica Kingsley Publishers.

Lawrence, C. (2008) *How to Make School Make Sense.* London: Jessica Kingsley Publishers.

Lawrence, C. (2010) *Successful School Change and Transition for the Child with Asperger Syndrome.* London: Jessica Kingsley Publishers.

Moyes, R.A. (2001) *Incorporating Social Goals in the Classroom: A Guide for Teachers and Parents of Children with High-Functioning Autism and Asperger Syndrome.* London: Jessica Kingsley Publishers.

Moyes, R.A. (2002) *Addressing the Challenging Behaviour of Children with High-Functioning Autism/Asperger Syndrome in the Classroom: A Guide for Teachers and Parents.* London: Jessica Kingsley Publishers.

Willey, L.H. (1999) *Pretending to be Normal: Living with Asperger's Syndrome.* London: Jessica Kingsley Publishers.

References

Asperger, H. (1991) 'Autistic Psychotherapy.' In U. Frith (ed.) *Autism and Asperger Syndrome*. Cambridge: Cambridge University Press.

Attwood, T. (1998) *Asperger's Syndrome: A Guide for Parents and Professionals*. London: Jessica Kingsley Publishers.

Attwood, T. (April 2000) *Should Children with an Autistic Spectrum Disorder be Exempted From Doing Homework?* Academic Paper. Available at www.tonyattwood.com, accessed on 20 February 2011.

Burgoine, E. and Wing, L. (1983) 'Identical triplets with Asperger's Syndrome.' *British Journal of Psychiatry 143.*

Edelson, S. (1995) '*Theory of Mind*.' Academic Paper written for Center for the Study of Autism, Salem, Oregon. Available at www.autism.com/fam_page.asp?PID=357

Fling, E.R. (2000) *Eating an Artichoke: A Mother's Perspective on Asperger's Syndrome*. London: Jessica Kingsley Publishers.

Grandin, T. (June 2001) *Teaching Tips for Children and Adults with Autism*. Academic Paper. Available at www.autism.com/ind_teaching_tips. asp

Gray, C. (1994) *Comic Strip Conversations*. Arlington, TX: Future Horizons.

Gray, C. (1997) *Social Stories and Comic Strip Conversations. Unique Methods To Improve Social Understanding*. Jenison, Michigan, MI: The Morning News.

Hall, K. (2000) *Asperger Syndrome, the Universe and Everything*. London: Jessica Kingsley Publishers.

Holliday Willey, L. (1999) *Pretending to be Normal: Living with Asperger's Syndrome*. London: Jessica Kingsley Publishers.

Hoopmann, K. (2001) *Blue Bottle Mystery: An Asperger Adventure.* London: Jessica Kingsley Publishers.

Ives, M. (1999) *What is Asperger Syndrome and How Will It Affect Me: A Guide For Young People.* London: The National Autistic Society.

Jackel, S. (June 1996) *Asperger's Syndrome – Educational Management Issues,* Academic Paper. Available at www.theparentaladvocate. com/aspergers.htm

Kirby, B. and Romanwski, P. (2001) *The OASIS Guide to Asperger Syndrome.* Arlington, TX: Future Horizons.

Leicester City Council Education Department and Leicestershire County Council Education Department (1998) *Asperger Syndrome – Practical Strategies for the Classroom: A Teacher's Guide.* London: The National Autistic Society.

National Autistic Society (2010) *Need to Know.* London: National Autistic Society. Available at www.autism.org.uk/en-gb/get-involved/campaign-for-change/our-campaigns/you-need-to-know/the-facts.aspx, accessed on 15 March 2011.

Websites

ASPEN (Asperger Syndrome Education Network)
www.aspennj.org

Asperger's Disorder Homepage
www.aspergers.com

Asperger Information Page
www.aspergerchronicles.net

Asperger Syndrome for Parents, Professionals and Educators
www.aspergersyndrome.com

Autism Resource Site
www.autism-resources.com

Ben's Asperger Room
http://xoomer.virgilio.it/marpavio/A_childrens_guide_to_Asperger_Syndrome.htm

Centre for the Study of Autism
www.autism.org

Educating the Student With Asperger Syndrome
www.aspennj.org/pdf/information/articles/educating-the-student-withasperger-syndrome.pdf

Families of Adults Afflicted with Asperger Syndrome
www.faaas.org

O.A.S.I.S.
www.aspergersyndrome.org

Tony Attwood
www.tonyattwood.com

Wrong Planet
www.wrongplanet.net

Resources

Applied Behaviour Analysis

Kearney, A.J. (2007) *Understanding Applied Behaviour Analysis: An Introduction to ABA for Parents, Teachers, and Other Professionals.* London: Jessica Kingsley Publishers.

Keenan, M., Henderson, M., Kerr, K.P. and Dillenburger, K. (2005) *Applied Behaviour Analysis and Autism: Building a Future Together.* London: Jessica Kingsley Publishers.

Newman, B., Reinecke, D., Birch, S. and Blausten, F. (2002) *Graduated Applied Behavior Analysis.* Dove and Orca.

Classroom Activities for Children with AS

Ansell, G.D. (2010) *Working with Asperger Syndrome in the Classroom: An Insider's Guide.* London: Jessica Kingsley Publishers.

Chinn, S. (2010) *Addressing the Unproductive Classroom Behaviours of Students with Special Needs.* London: Jessica Kingsley Publishers.

Martin, N. (2009) *Art as an Early Intervention Tool for Children with Autism.* London: Jessica Kingsley Publishers.

Rose, R. and Shevlin, M. (2010) *Count Me In!: Ideas for Actively Engaging Students in Inclusive Classrooms.* London: Jessica Kingsley Publishers.

Fiction

Hoopmann, K. (2000) *Blue Bottle Mystery: An Asperger Adventure.* London: Jessica Kingsley Publishers.

Hoopmann, K. (2001) *Of Mice and Aliens: An Asperger Adventure.* London: Jessica Kingsley Publishers.

Hoopmann, K. (2002) *Lisa and the Lacemaker: An Asperger Adventure.* London: Jessica Kingsley Publishers.

Hoopman, K. (2003) *Haze.* London: Jessica Kingsley Publishers.

Nichol, T. (2003) *Stephen Harris in Trouble: A Dyspraxic Drama in Several Clumsy Acts.* London: Jessica Kingsley Publishers.

Ogaz, N. (2002) *Buster and the Amazing Daisy.* London: Jessica Kingsley Publishers.

Victor, P. (2006) *Baj and the Word Launcher: Space Age Asperger Adventures in Communication.* London: Jessica Kingsley Publishers.

Social Stories

Al-Ghani, K.I. (2010) *Learning About Friendship: Stories to Support Social Skills Training in Children with Asperger Syndrome and High Functioning Autism.* London: Jessica Kingsley Publishers.

Gast, C. and Krug, J. (2007) *Caring for Myself: A Social Skills Storybook.* London: Jessica Kingsley Publishers.

Gray, C. and White, A. (2002) *My Social Stories Book.* London: Jessica Kingsley Publishers.

Visual Strategies

Bromley, K., Irwin-De Vitis, L. and Modlo, M. (1995) *Graphic Organizers: Visual Strategies for Active Learning.* New York, NY: Scholastic, Inc.

Hodgdon, L.A. (1995) *Visual Strategies for Improving Communication: Practical Supports for School and Home.* Troy, MI: Quirk Roberts Publishing.

McClannahan, L. and Krantz, P. (1999) *Activity Schedules for Children with Autism: Teaching Independent Behaviour (Topics in Autism)*. Bethesda, MD: Woodbine House.

Savner, J. and Myles, B. (2000) *Making Visual Supports Work in the Home and Community: Strategies for Individuals with Autism and Asperger Syndrome*. Shawnee Mission, KS: Autism Asperger Publishing Company.

Tarquin, P. and Walker, S. (1996) *Creating Success in the Classroom: Visual Organizers and How to Use Them*. Westport, CT: Libraries Unlimited.

Some Common
Conditions
Associated with
Asperger Syndrome

General

Hanks, R. (2010) *Common SENse for the Inclusive Classroom: How Teachers Can Maximise Existing Skills to Support Special Educational Needs.* London: Jessica Kingsley Publishers.

Kurtz, L.A. (2007) *Understanding Motor Skills in Children with Dyspraxia, ADHD, Autism, and Other Learning Disabilities: A Guide to Improving Coordination.* London: Jessica Kingsley Publishers.

Kutscher, M.L. (2005) *Kids in the Syndrome Mix of ADHD, LD, Asperger's, Tourette's, Bipolar, and More!: The One Stop Guide for Parents, Teachers, and Other Professionals.* London: Jessica Kingsley Publishers.

ADD/ADHD (Attention Deficit Disorder/Attention Deficit Hyperactivity Disorder)

Flick, G.L. (1997) *ADD/ADHD Behavior-Change Resource Kit: Ready-to-Use Strategies and Activities for Helping Children with Attention Deficit Disorder.* San Francisco, CA: Jossey-Bass Publishers.

Levine, M. (2002) *A Mind at a Time.* New York, NY: Simon & Schuster Publishers.

Munden, A. and Arcelus, J. (1999) *The ADHD Handbook: A Guide for Parents and Professionals.* London: Jessica Kingsley Publishers.

Steer, J. and Horstmann, K. (2009) *Helping Kids and Teens with ADHD in School: A Workbook for Classroom Support and Managing Transitions.* London: Jessica Kingsley Publishers.

Dysgraphia

Cavey, D.W. (2000) *Dysgraphia: Why Johnny Can't Write: A Handbook for Teachers and Parents (3rd Edition).* Austin, TX: Pro-Ed Publishers.

Olsen, J.Z. (1998) *Handwriting Without Tears (Teachers Edition, 7th Edition).* Potomac, MD: Handwriting Without Tears Publishers.

Dyslexia

Chivers, M. (2006) *Dyslexia and Alternative Therapies.* London: Jessica Kingsley Publishers.

Hultquist, A.M. (2006) *An Introduction to Dyslexia for Parents and Professionals.* London: Jessica Kingsley Publishers.

Hultquist, A.M. (2008) *What is Dyslexia?: A Book Explaining Dyslexia for Kids and Adults to Use Together.* London: Jessica Kingsley Publishers.

Stowe, C.M. (2000) *How to Reach and Teach Children and Teens With Dyslexia: A Parent and Teacher Guide to Helping All Ages Academically, Socially and Emotionally.* San Francisco, CA: Jossey-Bass Publishers.

Dyspraxia

Boon, M. (2010) *Understanding Dyspraxia: A Guide for Parents and Teachers (2nd Edition)*. London: Jessica Kingsley Publishers.

Drew, S. and Atter, E. (2008) *Can't Play Won't Play: Simply Sizzling Ideas to get the Ball Rolling for Children with Dyspraxia*. London: Jessica Kingsley Publishers.

Portwood, M. (1999) *Developmental Dyspraxia – Identification and Intervention: A Manual for Parents and Professionals (2nd Edition)*. London: David Fulton Publishers.

Echolalia/Tourette Syndrome

Chowdhury, U. and Robertson, M. (2006) *Why Do You Do That?: A Book about Tourette Syndrome for Children and Young People*. London: Jessica Kingsley Publishers.

Dornbush, M.P. and Pruitt, S.K. (1995) *Teaching the Tiger: A Handbook for Individuals Involved in the Education of Students with Attention Deficit Disorders, Tourette Syndrome or Obsessive-Compulsive Disorder*. Duarte, CA: Hope Press.

Robertson, M.M. and Baron-Cohen, S. (1998) *Tourette Syndrome: The Facts*. Oxford: Oxford University Press.

Shimberg, E.F. (1995) *Living With Tourette Syndrome*. New York, NY: Simon & Schuster Publishers.

NLD (Nonverbal Learning Disability)

Tanguay, P.B. (2002) *Nonverbal Learning Disabilities at School: Educating Students with NLD, Asperger Syndrome and Related Conditions*. London: Jessica Kingsley Publishers.

Thompson, S. (1997) *The Source for Nonverbal Learning Disorders* (formerly titled *I Shouldn't Have to Tell You! A Guide to Understanding Nonverbal Learning Disorders*). East Moline, IL: LinguiSystems Inc.á.

OCD (Obsessive Compulsive Disorder)

Derisley, J., Heyman, I., Robinson, S. and Turner, C. (2008) *Breaking Free from OCD: A CBT Guide for Young People and Their Families.* London: Jessica Kingsley Publishers.

Hyman, B.M. and Pedrick, C. (1999) *The OCD Workbook: Your Guide to Breaking Free from Obsessive-Compulsive Disorder.* Oakland, CA: New Harbinger Publishers.

Waltz, M. and Claiborn, J.M. (2000) *Obsession Compulsive Disorder: Help for Children and Adolescents.* Cambridge, MA: Patient-Centered Guides, A Division of O'Reilly & Associates, Inc.

Index